Hunger

Hunger

First published in Great Britain in 2015
by Mud Press ©

ISBN: 978-0-9934037-0-5

Printed by Books Factory
http://booksfactory.co.uk/

Hunger

edited by Georgina Wilding

Dean Atta Gabriel Jones Joshua Judson

Rosemary Swainston Joshua Jones Jim Hall

Carmina Masoliver Georgina Norie Ben Johnson

Chris McLoughlin

Mud Press was born out of defiance.
It's a s l y w a v e to anyone who says
poetry is
old,
boring
or dead.

Contents

Introduction

'Hunger', explains the Oxford English Dictionary, is 'a discomfort or weakness from lack of food; a desire or craving. To want very much', but as a primal force of nature, does it not do more than that? To me, hunger is drive, is erotic, is honesty, a necessary lie, death, tunnel vision, blurred vision, the clang of your partner's keys in the door – alright, yes, and pizza, it's pizza too.

But really, does hunger not cover the base of all human intent? I think, yes. Hunger was one of the very first themes that came to mind when I decided to run a poetry competition, because, as I mentioned, its roots lie in almost everything. I knew that this would create a breeding ground for creative genius, and allow for poems that represent emotionally integral and teeth grittingly human experiences from all walks of life.

The poets featured within this collection explore hunger by lifting up its carpet, scratching and sniffing at each stain, and pulling apart all the dust that has been swept underneath it, to create a visceral and poignant collection, that I could not be more proud of.

Georgina Wilding

March 2015

Dean Atta

Undetectable

I don't know if coffee is something I want to keep
drinking now I've given up drugs, alcohol, meat,
eggs and dairy. Vegan feels like a vain title. I feel
better taking this communion of coffee with soya.

It will be Christmas soon. Since that Boxing Day
bareback fuck, church has seemed as intimidating
as the sexual health clinic. This coffee is cold
and bitter now but I am the caffeine and Demerara

pulsing through my system. He told me he was HIV
positive but that it was undetectable. I didn't know
what that meant at the time; when I looked it up online
it made me think of God, laying dormant inside me.

Gabriel Jones

Hoops

I have a relationship with your earrings,
when I walk in to find you asleep
big head poking from duvet cocoon,
your left hoop vibrates a greeting.
An almost imperceptible hum,
a gold glint
a gypsy wink.

When I am lucky enough to find this scene
I put my index to my lips, signalling your
earrings not to let on, whereupon
they become still and
I tread like a burglar stealing seconds.
It's like you're asleep in my belly,
filling me up with warm recycled breaths
that smell of your mouth.
When enough air has been exhaled into me
I begin to rise.
Bobbing up, off-kilter and
if you were to wake at this point,
you would find a stray helium balloon in your room.
Your earrings always alert me however,
popping a tiny hole in my midriff
which fires me like a leaf
to and fro
until I slip into your bed
and swear your left hoop to secrecy.

Joshua Judson

On The Bus Home

We sit, not speaking
as if unsaid sentences
can fill our aching bellies.
Her hand claws my leg,
half hindering
like she's thinking about
tearing out a chunk and
taking a bloody bite.
I'm starving.
She nods a shared sensation.
For now, we're equal.
Two grumbling torsos
on the bus back to mine.

Rosemary Swainston

Razors Edge

The steam closes its elbows for her to hide behind.
She crouches into a butter bean shape:
awkward and glistening and drenched by the shower.
Choking on air, her heart slips straight through her
on to razor's edge that meet her legs gladly.
She will peel herself into something pinker.
As her husband peels his chin in mirrors
humming boy band tributes, unaware of her
eyes beating jackhammers onto his back.
She has been split in half by their neighbour Ken.
Who sucked her nipples like a hedge trimmer,
all because she was tired of dinner chats
over knife edges and sex that felt like planks.
All because she doesn't want to be his guitar string,
a faded dream. She tightropes across razor's edge.
Her skin no longer smooth still craves to be touched.

Joshua Jones

I, Hannibal

Cannibals don't eat their enemies,
we eat those we love.
And I really love you.
It's a particular type of love.
What I really crave is the affection you can give me.
I relish your praise in private,
and more so on Facebook,
where others can see my worthiness.
I take endless nibbles of your words and your touch.
I feast on your loyalty.
When you're done giving freely,
I manipulate you to give more.
I am the fat black spider sat in her web.
I consume the life in you and give little thought
to producing new life for you.
As my cherished intimate,
you have no more
dangerous enemy than I.

When I see you bequeath company to others,
I do not rejoice in your happy friendships.
I am jealous and hate you for it.
Love like that can be 90% hatred and still call itself love.

I will do extravagant acts of devotion for you
but only in anticipation that you will deliver back
in equivalent measure.
I've always felt on the outside of any side you could imagine.
You will be my bridge.

I embrace you tightly as I gasp
under a chronic undertow of loneliness.
You are my life jacket.
Now you sink with me.
I'll offer up sacrifices in worship to you
and we'll both be burned in unholy flame.

At some point during my consumption,
I will realise this is a futile meal.
The more I devour,
the more I'm disappointed.
I feast, but I keep getting hungry.
I am starving for a Saviour but
as I carve into your blood and flesh
it is I who am hollowed.

Jim Hall

Hunger: A Strong Desire Or Craving.

Or, your stomach. Its food-court collapse of KFC.
Mouth, a stuffed exhibit of fried chicken and yes.

Or, love in summer. Say apple juiced lips,
first kiss beneath the yellow tube slide,
her firefly-orange dress more miracle
than any sunset she chased you through.

Or, that song. Dropped in your ghost-town of a leaving party
& how the body moves to soak up the three minute spill.

Or, thirst for language. Despite seventeen texts,
the fourth glass of rum, your grasp of her shoulder in a taxi.

Or, your father. Folding away the wing mirror
instead of your loneliness
before sliding off each driving glove.

Or, despite the flat line of today:
the pulse of tomorrow. The
promise of new, of reach,
alive.

Your life, a full plate
& you?

Starving.

Carmina Masoliver

The Unlatching

House party pulling as many tongues as I could tug,
drunk, I asked if I was pretty enough. Before our date
he asked if I was the slutty one. Was I supposed to say yes?
Pressed bodies fully clothed, when all I asked to do was talk.
He spoke in imperatives, talk then, toilet tears, cards from his

girlfriend. I was his girlfriend and he never told his mum,
while he handcuffed me in plastic and I struggled to break free.
Told me to take off my clothes, so I polka dot dressed
the floor; on bed in bra and cotton knickers asked me
if I had any self respect. I thought this was foreplay

and I wanted it, waited for him drunk on wine and he came
after work, came all apologies. And I wouldn't have cared,
after years stacked up like these undeleted emails:
select all, enter – gone. That was our fate.
And I wouldn't have cared. But he said he'd lose respect
for me. And, well, if that were true, then more fool you.

I was true. And I will not apologise for believing the words
and misplaced musical notes wrapped round your neck.
I will not say sorry for meeting someone new after
repeated clichés down phone-lines. And I cannot admit
I'm crazy for knocking on your door just to know where I stand.

I will not regret the tears I cried, will not judge
myself for being young and naive and self-medicated.
I valued myself more than the boys I chose respected me,
didn't think slut was derogatory until it was aimed at me.
It was they who doused my body in shame. The only apologies
to myself, for the mistakes I made, for the unlatching.

Georgina Norie

i

Vulture

Addicted to picking at your corpse.
Believe me, I've tried to stop.
Raw strings of muscle
flounder in my teeth;
gentle technique with a toothpick is
required to ease them from these
tense places.

Help me, please, in this desert of your
death, incite a desire within to want to stop
scavenging for the life
you should have had.

Your liver, kidney and intestine
were green with cancer. I ate them.
Clamped them into my jaw and dared
the cells to multiply. They were already dead.

Lemon helped with the taste. You showed us which
meats improved with sharpness. The meat of you,
the decay of you. I'm still chewing.

ii

Fox

They say death slows down the digestive process by
approximately 5 years, and then it takes about
that long to compost.

When that soil is ready to use, Sweet Williams will sprout there,
pink and short and fragrantless.
One day I'll bring them back to the frames of our garden,
queues will form — children, the elderly, foxes will
dream into them.

To plant their seeds, I'll tug at weeds, green like intestines and cancer and
underneath I'll find your feet. Ready to dance again,
valiant, crumbling and brown.

Will you visit me then?
Show me how to walk without crumbling?
Help me to feast on the zest of your life instead
of the rind of your death.

Addicted to picking at your corpse.
Believe me, I'm trying to stop.

Ben Johnson

Adoption

The hedge's calling hunger, drove the black bird
through days which stretched away from equinox,
like worms he hauled from spring-rich flower beds
and hammered into numbness against the bricks.

From morning chorus through to twilight choir
he racked his beak with beetles and grubs,
shipping them back to yawning mouths and fighting wings,
as desperate to thrive as faith or love.

His endless journeys caught my short attention,
made me think beyond words or resting
about the balance of living against exhaustion
and the press of hours that are swiftly passing.

Then June, he brought his lad down from the nest
twice his size and brown with speckled breast.

Chris McLoughlin

Young Hunger

I place cigarette nineteen to my lips.

It's too risky to steal another round
of corned beef, ketchup and bread.
The flatmates are suspicious,

telling tales of the
Mystery of the Missing Meat.

Empty pockets,
even the jangling of my jacket
comes back tuneless,
drained by Mayfair's, Gin
and bad decisions.

I herd stray copper coins,
step onto pigskin cobblestones,
rotten cotton candy hair
stained by egg yolk streetlights
under a liquorice sky.

The shop fronts are asleep,
except the tired golden arches,
but my palm's too light.

The moon's silver reflection
a sunken coin in the river,
just out of reach.

A Commentary:
Inside the poems...

Undetectable

This is a poem that frightens me, not only because of how revealing I feel it is, but also because I tried to make it good. A lot of my poems write themselves, but this one didn't want to be written.

Hoops

My writing process is not always smooth. In this case, I went from being overwhelmed and wanting to write, to lying in bed oblivious of the person next to me, cradling my cold iPhone screen trying to communicate a memory.

This sums up my general process I think; when I'm inspired I'm upright, receptive and empathetic. My problem is this creative space seldom resembles the English language and after I say 'Gabriel, you definitely should make this into a poem' the pressure sooner or later throws me firmly back into my rational brain. I go from being fully in a moment; to lost in the new task of trying to find the best words to communicate it. I don't always find this very easy (cue: me, with my iPhone, trying to filter a memory into ill-fitting words). It's certainly never a case of flowing quills, red wine or mahogany. However one of my favourite ways to generate material is free-writing* which, for me, tends to produce more honesty, or a focus on something I wouldn't have necessarily chosen to write about. I think this piece had a simpler transition from brain to page than others, and for this reason I think it is more truthful.

* Trying to write non-stop for a set period of time without censoring.

On The Bus Home

I realised recently that almost all the art I like has two common denominators:
    1: Simplicity
    2: A sense of immediacy or urgency.

Nirvana, Kurt Vonnegut, Ernest Hemingway, DJ Premier: all these guys have a handle on a sort of edge-of-your-seat simplicity that really turns me on creatively.

The early 20th century movement of Imagist poetry seems to have a special relationship with immediacy and simplicity. And it's for this reason, I think, that Imagism has been the cartridge in the game boy of my writing approach for the last few months.

Imagist poems are really good for capturing moments, those fleeting instances of coincidence and magic that a camera just couldn't hold. 'On The Bus Home' is an attempt at one such moment.

It's one of them where a connection between two people is so strong, so heavy in the air, that the people involved need not address it. It's just there.

Razors Edge

This poem had originally started as an exercise set by Mr Stephen Fry in his brilliant book, *An Ode Less Travelled*. Before I read this book I had barely written with any structure at all, but he was keen for his readers to count syllables and think about where to put emphasis on words. Of course as the poem got re-edited it lost its ten syllable per line structure and probably the rhythmic pattern I'd originally attempted, but it was fun. Not sure where the content came from, I won't tell you if it was based on anyone I know. I was just in the shower and really wanted to write the line about the steam closing its elbows so mostly it started from there!

I, Hannibal

I'm not comfortable admitting that a cannibal lives inside me. But it would be lying to say there's no truth to it.

Since first watching Anthony Hopkin's portrayal of Hannibal Lecter in Silence of the Lambs, the subject of real cannibalism has interested me. I wondered then if cannibalism wasn't just the rare abnormality of a psychopath, but rather a behaviour rooted in something far more human. Those who research are usually surprised that – contra Lecter – cannibals don't actually eat people they think rude or despicable. They cannibalise those they cherish or respect. That's why they eat them; they want the virtue of their meal to flow into them. They truly 'love' their food.

It is with that knowledge that I quiver when I catch myself loving a friendship more than I love the friend – when I care for what a person can give me more than their well-being. It's then that my inner cannibal begins to show his teeth. I hunger for some relationships to be deeper or more dynamic than they are. I am willing to give a lot. But I look for that attention to be reciprocated - and can be too easily wounded when it isn't. The longing to connect with another in deep affection isn't bad. This hunger can be satiated in healthy ways - but there's a potential darkness which lurks among the shards of our human brokenness. It is this spectre which I must prayerfully battle - lest it bring ruin to me and the one I love. If I make any relationship a god, it soon becomes a devil. It is that darkness that I am writing about and - in so naming it – hope to have some freedom from.

It is my ambition to write a book on the subject within the next year. News of this will be available on my blog: JoshuaDJones.com.

Hunger: A Strong Desire or Craving

Hunger may first make us think of a next meal. The want to fill an empty stomach. Perhaps little more than a sprawling food court, as much as the possibility of a first bite of bread in days. A just — opened buffet. That first munch of the apple you kept in your satchel just in case. When I came to write something with the prompt of hunger I, too, began inside a food court, a KFC's teasing yes.

And yet.

As the poem found its feet I found myself exploring hunger as a more internal, guttural sensation. Something that shakes us awake amidst the sleepiest year. That which we yearn to satisfy not merely for the sake of our bellies, but perhaps the good of our lives. Maybe that hunger to reclaim youth, a brief kiss with a girl in a summer dress at thirteen whose memory you struggle to swallow. Maybe that hunger to leave behind your body when the right song comes on. Maybe that hunger to say exactly what you need to before your friend leaves the taxi, the night, behind. Maybe that hunger to have your father hold you instead of everything but you.

Maybe there is a hunger somewhere inside each of us, pushing us to not simply 'get through' another day but instead choose to claim it as our own.

Unlatching

This poem used the title 'The Unlatching' as a response from Muse Arcade, a communal online poetry writing exercise. An early draft was put out digitally with an anthology of work as part of my poetry collective, *Kid Glove*. One of the most valuable parts of writing for me is to get feedback, and it was great to work with Georgina as an editor, responding to her suggestions.

The idea behind the poem was to explore female heterosexuality, double standards, power relations, and the messy mix of alcohol that can often act as lubricant for teenage sexual exploration. I wanted the piece to be empowering for women, to reassert that it is society that creates this sexual shame, rather than the acts themselves. There's an idea that there's something wrong with you if you're a woman who is honest about sex. I feel that we shouldn't place shame on ourselves for being sexually liberated, and that the only mistake is to place trust in those who are not on that level, who still prescribe to the idea that a woman who is promiscuous is a 'slut' and yet a man can take pride in this behaviour. It's complicated, because I don't necessarily think it's healthy to binge drink and have multiple sexual partners, but it's the inequality I'm addressing here. I think it's important to be mindful that it's all part of a learning experience and you shouldn't be punished by others or by yourself for the past, whether you see it personally as a mistake or not.

I grew up going to a single-sex school, listened to songs like Christina Aguilera's *Can't Hold Us Down*, Destiny's Child's *Independent Women* and Hole's *Violet*. I was also inspired by visual artists such as Tracey Emin, Sarah Lucas and Shirin Nashat. I guess going to a single-sex school, you're sheltered from the world in some ways. I came out of this bubble at sixteen and wasn't expecting to be faced with boys who viewed women as objects, who reinforced the virgin/whore di-chotomy, and genuinely held up these sexual double standards.

This is for my girls all around the world
who have come across a man that don't respect your worth
thinking all women should be seen and not heard.
So what do we do girls? Shout out loud!
Letting 'em know were gonna stand our ground,
so lift your hands high and wave 'em proud.
Take a deep breath and say it loud –
never can, never will,
can't hold us down.

-Christina Aguilera

Vulture

It took a couple of years for the grief of my mum's death to rise into my consciousness; naturally it became the focus of my writing. As time went on, I started feeling like her passing and my loss were the only fuel I had to write with, like I was addicted to the despair. This poem served as a release for those emotions.

Adoption

A few years ago we moved into a house with a garden which was an exciting change for me as my previous homes were on managed estates. The first year was mostly spent in the garden growing vegetables and planting flowers. During this time a female blackbird adopted us and used to come and sit with us when she had time. Mostly she and her mate seemed rushed off their feet pulling worms from the garden and flying off with them. It was later in the season that we discovered why.

It was a very fruitful year poem wise with many featuring the life around us. An early version of this poem appeared on the forum *Poets' Graves* in 2009. The feedback was that the first stanza was okay, but the rest fell down. Punctuation was also an issue in places. At the time the poem was still too fresh for me to really edit it and I put it aside for later.

That later was a post on Facebook looking for poems on the theme of hunger. Somehow this recalled my still unedited draft. Time is a great way to gain new perspective on a poem and I could see that this poem was very weak and needed more than just a tweak. In the end I mostly rewrote the last three stanzas and felt much happier by the result.

We named the female blackbird Mela on account of her love for meal worms. Mela came back to us for three years running and it was great to see her in the spring, we would whistle and she would come flying straight over. Her mate never liked her being friendly with us and used to spend his spare time calling to her to get away from us.

Young Hunger was born on 12th December 2014, in the little town of Beeston. His father, Chris Mcloughlin, was working at the time as a poet, but Young never knew his mother. Young was brought into this world by the powers of the Free-Write (an exercise involving writing for ten minutes without stopping).

During his adolescence, Young was home-schooled by his father, with some additional lessons from local wordsmith Sarah Crutwell. These early years focussed on removing the extra lines that weren't necessary, making Young more powerful. This was followed by a rigorous training period, somewhere in the mountains of Tibet. Here, he went through twelve trials, or rewrites, before emerging as the figure he is known as today. Young Hunger now resides within the anthology you are currently holding, waiting for a reader in peril.

His father, Chris McLoughlin, disappeared soon after the extensive training. Some say he spontaneously combusted, creating a second big bang and therefore a new, mini universe, inside a plastic bag stuck in a tree on a windy day. Others are convinced he morphed into a hollow mountain slightly bigger than Everest, and now rests over Everest like a snug flat cap. So, you see that there mountain they're climbing? Yeah, that ain't Everest, that's Chris-verest.

The odd conspiracy nut says he currently resides within Nottingham, is a member of the poetry collective *Mouthy Poets*, and is completing his Masters in Creative Writing at the University of Nottingham.

I guess we'll never know…

About the poets

Dean Atta is a writer, performance poet and graduate of the Writer/Teacher MA at Goldsmiths College, University of London. He has been commissioned to write poems for Keats House Museum, National Portrait Gallery, Tate Britain and Tate Modern. His debut collection *I Am Nobody's Nigger* was published by The Westbourne Press in 2013 and was shortlisted for the Polari First Book Prize 2014. Atta lives in London and works internationally.

Gabriel Jones is a 23 year old from Aberystwyth in west Wales. Currently studying towards an Anthropology and Sociology BA in London and attempting to put experiences into poems, scripts and spoken word. An all-round tea enthusiast who often drinks pints of earl grey and a lover of stories, music and humans.

Joshua Judson was born in Reading, grew up in the Lake District and was made in Nottingham. He is studying Performance and Creative Enterprise at Guildhall School of Music and Drama, and runs Poetry Is Dead Good, a monthly poetry event at Jamcafé in Nottingham. Influences include Pusha T and Samuel Beckett.

Rose Swainston is a training Youth Worker who spends most of her days encouraging young people to enjoy literature. She originally began as a play-writer with several performances of her script *Obsidere* being premiered at SOHO theatre. Over the last year and a half she has been part of the Roundhouse collective and is now a resident artist with the newly named collective Kid Glove. Together they have performed all over the country and hope this will continue in the coming months.

Joshua Jones battles dragons while his Scandinavian wife, Irdi, builds castles. He likes music, friends, books, God, butter, his family and meat... in no particular order. He has written poetry since he was a teenager but only got involved in the Mouthy Poets collective after encouragement from a friend to develop his writing more. He is happy to be contacted for spoken word events or the slaying of dragons.

Jim Hall: A writer and educator working to uncover the silences we smuggle. Or, boy trying to claw out heart with pen. Or, a fistful of page in one hand, yours in the other.

Flawsfoldedtoorigamiswans.tumblr.com

Carmina Masoliver is an English Literature graduate from the University of East Anglia. Following graduating, she studied an MA in Creative Entrepreneurship, but now works in East London as an Academic Mentor for English. In her spare time she runs an event called *She Grrrowls* which features women in the arts. She also edits an anthology called *Poetry&Paint*. Carmina is a member of the *Burn After Reading* community and the *Kid Glove* collective. Her first poetry pamphlet was published in 2014 by Nasty Little Press, and she has performed at festivals including Latitude, In the Woods, and Bestival.

www.carminamasoliver.com
www.poetryandpaint.wordpress.com
www.shegrrrowls.tumblr.com

Georgina Norie is a London based poet with a keen interest in the therapeutic potential of creative writing. She explores her personal experiences of loss, love and womanhood using stark imagery and painful honesty, taking inspiration from both the maternal and the grotesque.

Ben Johnson is a New Milton-based poet with work previously published in; Ink, Sweat and Tears, Ghazal Pages, Kwartalnik and Antiphon. In 2013 Ben was one of three poets to win the Fermoy International Poetry Prize and more recently his poem 'Selkie' was Most Highly Commended in the Bristol Poetry Prize 2015.

Chris McLoughlin is a Nottingham based Poet and Fiction writer. He is currently studying MA Creative Writing at the University of Nottingham, and is a member of the Poetry Collective, Mouthy Poets. Chris is currently preparing his first poetry pamphlet.

You can find out more at:

YouTube channel 'Chris McLoughlin – Poetry'.

www.mouthypoets.com/need-a-poet/chris

www.noumena.org.uk/author/chrismc

About the editor

Georgina Wilding can knit mice and sandwiches, amidst other adorably useless objects. This, of course, puts to use her first class degree in Creative and Professional writing. She lives with her cat, Ivy, and many many plants. Her favourite colour is yellow, she's a member of the Mouthy Poets and she still owes her Grandad £20.

Acknowledgements

Thank you to everyone who spread the word about this competition, and about Mud Press in general; be it through passing out flyers, tweeting, posting, sharing — and of course by good old word of mouth.

Special thanks to *Riah*, who spent many a late night with me battling over flyer designs and Photoshop. To *Josh*, my second opinion on everything, all the way through. To *Kathryn*, for all her patience and hard work on her incredible cover design, alongside *Angelica* who is the smartest and most exciting graphic designer I know. To *Craig*, for always being a Tech God. To *Fardad*, Real Creative Futures and NBV for holding my hand. And of course to *Cathy*, who spent hours listening to me rant about screw posts and grams per square metre, and without whom none of this would have been possible.

This collection was first gathered and put together for my final year project at The University of Nottingham, but it is so much more than just a project. It is a pilot, the beginning, the proverbial first step towards building the foundations of Mud Press, and I can't thank everyone who has been involved enough, for getting me, and the dream, this far.

- Georgina Wilding

This anthology is dedicated to David Kershaw. Teacher, flash-mob dancer, friend and grammar God. His feedback and encouragement is what helped the idea of Mud Press come to life, and I can speak not only for myself, but for all of his students, when I say that our hearts are a little bit emptier without him.

Rest in peace, David.